NONE OF US ARE PROMISED TOMORROW

NONE OF US ARE PROMISED TOMORROW

Stations of the Mind
(Talking To Cancer)

LEE WARNER

POCAMUG PRESS™

Pocamug Press™
May's Lick, Kentucky
pocamug.com

Version 5/31/17

Copyright © 2016 Lee Warner
Edited by Michael H. Dickman
Cover photo ©2016 Lee Warner

Library of Congress Control Number: 2016958770

Odd Duck Editions
ISBN: 978-0-9908877-6-8

In remembrance of Randy Lee Kitchen

DEDICATION

This book is dedicated to all who have fought the fight with cancer. Whether you won or not, nobody will ever understand the feelings that you have had throughout your journey.

It is also a thank you to the many people who have stood beside me. They may not have understood the way I chose to do things; but I did it my way. Because all of us who has ever been through cancer—whether you or someone you know—we felt like we still needed to be in control of our lives. We may have been hard-headed silent but it was for our own sanity. We did things in a way that we felt kept us strong.

To my mom and dad: You both gave me an understanding of life and love. I learned so much from you two. I own so much to you all. Neither of you will ever know how important you are to me. I love you mom and dad.

To my children Randy, Brandon, and Matthew Dixon: I live every day for you three. I love you all so much. You have been my whole world ever since the day you were born. All three of you have made my life wonderful.

Many thanks over to Jim Warner who made my wild imaginations come to life. If I envisioned it he could build it. He always said I was sassy and didn't take no bull from anyone. Quite right he was.

Thanks a million Laura Weingartner, you're a gem of a friend. We are definitely quirky in a great way.

To Don Jones for helping me keep my spirit alive, even when others were looking at me with disgust, pity, or sorrow. He didn't. Our interest in guns, toilet paper, prep shopping and peanut butter milkshakes would make you shake your head.

No matter who I was out and about with: None of them will ever be able to forget my wild wacky socks and my energetic sense of humor.

To Jackye Jones who never looked at me like I had cancer: We sang in the isles of Walmart and had wonderful conversations. I was so happy when she found her green thumb.

To my family and friends who sent inspirational words and beautiful pictures, I thank you. My thanks I give back to you in words. I astounded many with my writing. It made them either scratch their head or it gave them hope.

Hail and love to my COFFEE! Without it nobody would have survived being around me.

A Goddess' tiger has a smile that is worth a thousand words and the golden nectar shall always live within you forever.

To the women in my life: Thanks for sharing in these wonderful and weird moments brought to you by yours truly.

Editor's Note

In editing Lee's words I have used a light touch. This is partly due to her own request, and partly because of her creative, idiosyncratic use of language in this document. For example, I wrestled a bit with her phrase "spouts of leukemia" and then left it unchanged, as "spouts" appears to be a portmanteau of "spells and bouts" but also includes the sense of a stream of great force. There are other examples throughout the manuscript. Lee's pain, frustrations, tenacity, and enthusiasm for life fairly burst through the page from her poetic lines.

Chronic lymphocytic leukemia is classified as "rare" in that there are fewer than 200,000 US cases per year. It tends to affect those over forty rather than younger people. There is great promise in the techniques of genetic and immunological treatment; it is to be hoped that in a not-too-distant future, chemotherapy for all cancer will be a forgotten medical episode. To those still needing to undergo it, take heart from Lee's work: you are not alone.

Michael H. Dickman
October, 2016

INTRODUCTION

Since 2003, I have gone through many spouts with leukemia. I was diagnosed with CLL, chronic lymphocytic leukemia.

The American Cancer Association states:

Leukemia is different from other types of cancer that start in organs like the lungs, colon, or breast and then spread to the bone marrow. Cancers that start elsewhere and then spread to the bone marrow are not leukemia.

What is chronic leukemia?

Whether leukemia is acute or chronic depends on whether most of the abnormal cells are immature (and are more like stem cells) or mature (and are like normal white blood cells). In chronic leukemia, the cells can mature partly but not completely. These cells may look fairly normal, but they are not. They generally do not fight infection as well as normal white blood cells do. The leukemia cells survive longer than normal cells, and build up, crowding out normal cells in the bone marrow. Chronic leukemia can take a long time before it causes problems, and most people can live for many years. But chronic leukemia is generally harder to cure than acute leukemia.

In others words Ode to the flippin' Joy. But I am still here and I still carry with me my sensational sarcastic humor. This has been a tough journey. There will never be a day that has the same feelings when we are dealing with cancer. Stations of the Mind started out as my own personal journey.

I was advised by a nurse to start a journal of how I felt. She said it doesn't matter whether you are having a good day or a bad day, it helps you to get your emotions off your chest.

The only words that came to my head was, I HATE F'ING CANCER. Not a day went by that I didn't write. This journal carries my expressions of hate, pain, tears, disappointments and love for life.

Some days I was a complete mess. I remember some days feeling I was trapped on an emotional roller coaster and the only way out was down. Many times I was ready to say, to hell with the treatments and all the medicines. I wanted to walk away as if I didn't have cancer, which is the mentality that many of us have. I didn't want to be a burden on anyone, so I would fight every single stinking day through this demise of misery. I would cry all the flippin' time when I would try to do things around the house. My body would just give out. There would be days on end that I would lie in bed unable to get up, but somehow I did it. There was a constant fight going on in my head of what I used to do versus what I couldn't do anymore. Everyone who has gone through cancer and treatments knows exactly what I am talking about. It really does suck.

The good days were the days I wrote mesmerizing words that shocked so many people who kept up with me through this nightmare. But to those who were going through the same thing, they understood all too well.

Just know that there were days I didn't know if I was going to live from one day to the next. Those were the days I didn't share how I felt with anyone. There wasn't much I felt like doing while sick. The good days were like a yo-yo. I would try to play music on my keyboard, or read, which is precisely why my house began to look like a library. Crocheting became valuable to me, so much in fact that in 2006 I crocheted a queen-size blanket for my mother. She still uses it to this day.

It's funny the things you think about when you live your life with one foot in the dark and one foot in the grey.

Someone said to me, "You mean when you live your life in the dark or the light."

I said "No, I meant grey."

The reason I always said grey was because I was closer to death than most were. As horrible as I felt, God did not take me and I would get angry. I would cry out and ask, "Why did you leave me here?" I was ready to go. I couldn't take any more. This was the side that nobody saw but they could tell through my writings that I was utterly bitter. Though some of the journal entries may not make any sense to you, they are not supposed to. I was describing how I was feeling or my view of pictures that friends sent to me. Some were dark, cold and perhaps full of hate, while some were funny and didn't make sense. But you have to understand, I was done dealing with cancer and some days I found no hope.

This journal made me think about how our thought processes work. Especially when we can go for being completely outraged to peace and quiet. In terms, most people usually have between 60,000 to 80,000 thoughts a day, 2000 to 3300 an hour, to about 48.6 thoughts a minute. Some of you are probably thinking that is how I spent my days. My answer to this would be: You are right—but so do you. With that being said, I present to you *None of Us Are Promised Tomorrow: Stations of the Mind*.

Lee Warner
October 2016

PART ONE
ONE FOOT IN THE DARK,
ONE FOOT IN THE GREY

Not Always
Patience is not always a virtue, it is sometimes just a kick in the ass. So don't tell me to have patience.

Don't Believe In the Juice
V8 juice doesn't fix everything.

A War of Three
There is a fine line between love, hate, and depression. It's a constant tug of war that will kick your derrière all the time.

Rum You Say
Depressed? you ask. Nope, but pass the rum just in case. Because the pain meds stop working.

Crossed Wire
I am your light. Oh wait, never mind. I've got a wire loose.

Smile Sunshine

Rude people irritate me. You can say hello to be nice and yet they are still rude as can be. So perhaps we need to blow a little bit of sunshine up your ass. Then you might not be so rude. You may actually radiate kindness and blossom a smile. Just don't hurt yourself. Too much kindness all at once may cause you to blow up.

When The Meds Begin

You're not annoying. You are just blissfully crazy in the world of insanity.

Lost Without Understanding

Isn't she pretty said the blind man who lost his dog.

Carry Disinfectant Spray

Who the hell wants to use a public bathroom when you're sick. Public bathrooms are like mines that got the shaft.

Too Late
Time to find the umbrella, after you are already caught in the rain. Why does it always rain when I have to go to my oncologist?

Bathroom Counter Needed
If you haven't got anything better to do today: You can come here and keep track of how many times I have had to occupy the john.

Bathroom Humor
I feel so lovely that I shall have my coffee in the throne room this morning.

That's The Way To Lift The Spirit
There is nothing like trying to take your mind off of things. So you listen to the radio, only to hear the announcer say, "It's going to be another messed up weekend."

Mine
I don't need your attitude. I have one of my own, thank you.

Nurse Requirement

I want to know, are nurses trained to lie to you? I mean is there a course they must take? "How to lie to your cancer patients 101." Spare me the BS!

Dim Day

When you feel like the sunshine is gone, turn on the damn light!

Hula Lost

I have lost my hula in the hoop a long time ago.

Lesson of Needles Needed

Me, doctors, nurses and needles are not cooperating very well today. I think they need a lesson in—YOU'RE NOT DIGGING FOR GOLD! DOES THE WORD GENTLE MEAN ANYTHING TO YOU?

Infliction

Bee stings firing into dry veins, prevails the loathsome infliction, as the smile grows dim. The vibrations of fire from the meds awaken the royal colors of the earth, enriching the light in my eyes as I all too soon, shall feel no pain.

Peace

Though there is uncertainty in my life, I felt serenity like that of a delicate breeze, I am at peace.

Somatic Pain of Cancer

Pain disturbs the sleep. While others are snuggled in their warm blankets the envy of sleep dominates the mind because the body cannot rest. I revel in the picturesque of the sunset. I wait and watch the peace dipping behind the hills, as it prepares the earth to sleep, until the sun rises. For some it is not like that. Reality sets in; a horrid nightmare is revealed as the shadows under the eyes become more sinister. There is no escape from the torturous somatic sensation that many cannot understand. Once touched by the poison that was created by man, the body becomes damaged. Though we try to make ourselves think that we are unassailable, it doesn't help. It is because we are fighting between letting go and trying to stay.

Train of Longing Reprieve

Deprived of sleep because of the pain. The low sound of the train's horn comforts my ears, in an almost eerie way. I try to set forth my mind on other things as I hear the train upon its tracks. Longing to take that ride in the hopes of finding solace and sleep. I try yet again to close my eyes and listen as the train drifts away. All the while wondering if the pain will evanesce and depart. This is when the darkness becomes more real.

Applesauce Delusions

The first moron who said you should take your meds with applesauce to make it easier to swallow, was apparently delusional. I found it is like trying to swallow a locust wrapped in sticky tape.

The Path of Life

Sometimes life isn't fair. I feel like I have had

curve balls thrown at me. It doesn't mean that I have given up. It just means this fight is getting harder to hold onto. Many who are going through the same thing understand this. We know life is precious, but you never know when our last words will be our last.

A Shadow of Hope

The locks become shorter. Once a blossoming flower, now droops in the rain. Time is shadowed by pain. They say to be strong. They know not what they ask. Shadows under the eyes reveal the restless and sleepless nights, but yet hope remains.

Cancerous Torments

Why is it that we feel like we are cascading from the world of light into the bowels of a treacherous burning torment, until the body fights beyond its strength or gives into drained veins? This is a story that many will never know and I pray they never will. Darkness shadows my body like static cling. There is always the cruel taste of bile, blood and iron, upon my tongue and in my mouth, always brought upon by the medicine of man. It is meant to heal the body, but yet destroys it at the same time. The question is whether thy will is stronger than thy poison.

Grey Silence
One foot that was in the light now walks in the grey and the dark. Silence is your reward.

Silent Bell Tower
For no bell tower, whether great or small shall ring under the silence of the dawn.

Fight To Believe
Sometimes your mind is fighting to believe that miracles can happen.

Bad Day
There are just days I feel like shyt and life becomes more than I can take.

Velcro Wig Testing

It is a good day to try out the Velcro against the wind experiment. Cha-ching—it was a success.

Tattered

As I held the tattered box of hospital bracelets in my hands, I realized I was alone. There is a fine line between love and hate, in which neither I felt at that moment. Until I overheard what others were thinking, when they saw this bald woman with only a scarf on her head. It was there when I felt the cold stings of hate, due to the demise of human decency and humanity. I felt like a tattered shirt, ripped by the ignorance of other people's vanity. I could feel my compassion being plucked away.

LW (Lee Warner) Proverbs

Sometimes what the heart knows the head forgets. Stupid comes in many forms. Pride steps in the way and provides ignorance.

Conglomerate Soaring

The mind is a conglomerate of numerous mental images that sometimes just needs a glass of brandy and a poisoned IV drip. This will allow my mind to empathize the vast and colorful perspectives that set the soul soaring.

If I Stay

If I stay is all I can say. Not that it's really my choice at this point. I know you cannot understand how I am feeling or what this is like. It was supposed to be a good day, but it turned bad and yet again the pain is more than I can stand. It is as if the music of life is still, with only my heartbeat in my ear. All you really want to do is scream at the top of your lungs— F%CK THIS! JUST LET ME DIE ALREADY!

P.S. You bring out my immortal beauty. Finally able to enjoy the flounderous swirls in my head.

…The medicine that oncologists give their patients can bring relief and strange visions…

Madness Is You

Someone said to me. You complained before about how you went through leukemia at certain points in your life and you felt by yourself, now you complain that people are just in your face. Cancer makes you feel like shyt. You are either up and trying to be hopeful or you're down in the flippin' dumps. I didn't shadow myself into my own madness. CANCER DID THAT FOR ME!

Inevitable

Sometimes the inevitable will happen and there is nothing we can do. Don't let your last words be silence.

Awaiting the Wings

Immaculate wings touched by grace await for thee. Pristine and white, fly whether it is day or night. From the heavens they shall descend. Swooping down they shall attend to the weak and the sick, wrapping them with the solace of love, as they await the voice that shall instruct them to ascend back to the heavens above.

I Waited For You

I waited to see you. I waited for you so that you could tell me that everything was going to be all right. Each day became worse and worse and I became afraid. I wasn't afraid of dying. I was afraid that I would never see you. I had never felt so damn alone. I wanted to give up. I became bitter and didn't want to continue with any more chemo, radiation or pain medicine. I wanted to say to hell with everything, I'm done. I felt like it was my fault that cancer fell upon me. I cried so much because I started to hate life and yet you still never came. I wanted to die. But after months of going through all the lovely things that comes with cancer, God had another plan. Not only did he advance me into remission, he brought you before me, to see that I was still here.

Kicking A Flake

Right now I feel like I'm trying to kick a field goal with a snow flake.

Smile For Others

I did not feel the smiles that I gave. They never came easy. I tried to overshadow my pain by smiling for others. I tried to keep my spirits up when I was around people so they would not feel uncomfortable. Truth be told, you don't know what to say to someone who has cancer and is fighting for their life.

Imminent Void

I am but a shell that remains empty from prior horrors of the past. Solitude of confinements trapped inside, longing to break free; not allowed to soak up the rays of the sun because of the cancer medicines. The nightmare remains as I fight each day to break away from the hellish horrible dreams of being on fire; caused by the poison that was being delivered into my veins.

Plausible Wish

We never know when our last good day will be. I wished for many good days on end. Inexhaustible pain persists without any assuage because of the leukemia. Which means in turn, the last good day is not as plausible as one wishes.

Hospital Tyrants

Oh yay! I thought—as if I had all the blood in the world to give, while watching the drops of my life dripping onto the floor and Bertha Big Shot blowing veins everywhere. Apparently blind, she had to call in Sister Sue Better Than You. Who tells you that you need to lay still. Are you kidding me lady? Big Bertha already blowed three veins and I am looking as if I have been in a boxing match with a sumo wrestler. You wait when I get better. I am calling a rematch. BLOODY TYRANTS!

PART TWO
FEELING BETTER

The Power of Writing Became my Talisman

As my body started going into remission, I found I was having more days where I felt alive. I still wasn't able to do many activities for a long period of time. The moments I had, brought about something I never thought about doing.

I found, through all of that pain and anguish, the power of writing. I found I could write words that could touch the darkest of souls. Writing became my euphoria.

I found I wanted to share my happy thoughts as I was becoming healthier and more alive. But more importantly, I wanted to share what it is like to be a person who found a renewal in life.

I take nothing for granted and I am as bold as ever.

What I discovered more appealing was my humor and sass, which definitely spilled over into my writing. Though there are entries that have no pictures, I hope you will be able to feel the vibration of my words so they too will become vivid and alive in your thoughts.

Ashes to Phoenix

When this is finished. I shall rise up from the ashes and fly high as a renewed Phoenix. I shall live life to the fullest.

Undiluted

The royals of my writing is magnanimous into the unfiltered mind. Perceived by only a few who can understand the astuteness that pen and paper can divulge. Undiluted parchment thirsts for my lyrical passage.

Emotionally Happy Tomorrow

When you feel emotionally happy, you feel good. You feel as if you can accomplish anything. It is important that people dealing with cancer are emotionally happy as well as physically. We are not looking for sympathy. We are simply trying to deal with the hand we have been dealt. Not only are we dealing with stares and being talked about. We are dealing with pain that is the emotional pain brought on by others. It is a shame how well I know this feeling. Those are the days

I prefer to just stay in my house behind closed doors. It doesn't matter whether you tell us to ignore what others say because the damage has already been done. Lifting our spirits is one of the best gifts that you can offer. Be supportive because one day we may not be here. None of us are promised tomorrow.

Ethereal of Life

Writing comes as natural as breathing for me. Many people do not know how to express themselves or take the time to marvel in the ethereal of life's simplicity. Every day holds a certain exhilaration for me. It has come from within the sadness I have had to endure from being sick and recovering. Given another chance for reflexion for words that sometimes touches the very soul of others. There is an unfathomable light that shines within me. A light for the expressions of our lives that makes us who we are but only so few get to experience. I revel in the words that come from my heart to give to others in hopes that in some small way it may bring forth a smile into your day.

I had many friends who would send me pictures of their vacations or places they had been. Some caught on that I was writing and asked if I would come up with an inscription for a picture that they took. Unfortunately they didn't want to relinquish their photos, which I understand. Therefore many of the excerpts in Part Two are my feelings when I looked upon certain photographs or my own outings. Just the same I hope you enjoy.

Morning Thoughts
Slipping into the depths of tranquility engaged with the thoughts that only the lifting fog will know.

Beacon
The euphonious light beacons through the ardent passions of the splendiferous sunset.

Irrevocable Essence
Irrevocable contentment shines whether the

dusk has come or the dawn has risen. Candescent yearning is bestowed in reminiscence of how we want to encounter the essence of another's aspiration.

The Ocean's Intrigue
The tantalizing salt water stimulates the senses and our eyes become intrigued with picturesque scene, while your mind relishes and reflects on how someone's words can touch your soul.

Skies Ablaze
The exalted bronze skies euphoria trifles the malleable grey hues of dusk.

Grey Light
One foot in the light shadowed by one foot in the grey. As we look upon the toppling of God's creation, we realize we too are his creations.

Aesthetical Grace
Many shades of grey are sometimes our lives but as we look into the sky, heaven radiates the aes-

thetic grace murmuring the instructions that only some may hear.

Prisms Not Paint
Mirrored ruminations of the intricate swirls look back at themselves with admiration. Colors reflecting their own prisms that not even paint can mimic.

A Capella Eclipse
The moon is as clear as an eclipse that filters a lighted path that only your senses can barely coincide with the *a capella*-ness inside your head.

Lunate Observer
Lunation articulates the apparatus of the Sun, bringing the tranquility into the heart and soul of the observer.

Nature's Symphony
Ardour of Dominicus ablazed by the tranquility of the ocean's binary compound. Transforms fire and water into a collaborated symphony.

Panoptic Sheath

As weathering as the attributes of nature can be, there too is life. Renewing its sheath beneath a panoptic of wood.

Achromatic Waves

Time is reflected as it stands still beneath the glassy, cool waves of the achromatic water.

Perceived Lineage

The blue lineage of God has many paths and angles to the soul. Perceived by his children his shadow is cast to the right side of the light… that only he can provide and is seen by so few.

Ascending Blue

As the night ascends, we are gifted with a lustrous spectral of the bluest of blue. Awaiting to slumber us into the most sensual tranquility of dreams as we begin our itinerary to remission.

Writing Your Own World

Sometimes you just got to write your own world because nobody understands you better than yourself. This Journey, this story is no longer under the rug. The fear, hate and tears that others bestowed upon me when I was down, made me want to look them in the eye and say shame on you. Where was their true down-home goodness? Perhaps their manners sank to the bottom of the toilet. But I rose above their cruelness with the return of a flipped bird and a sass in my step. Because if cancer didn't kill me then neither can their words.

Because I found that I loved writing so much, I saved this entry for last. Which in turn should tell you that I shall continue writing until my blind dog comes home.

Just One Writing Goal

My proclivity for writing has inspired me to be one of the most beautiful asinine writers of my time. So enjoy the sometimes provocative invocations that will leave you scratching your head or cause you to drink. Whichever it leads you to. Just enjoy it.

AFTERWORD

Throughout this process I have gone into remission for the time being. However, when you are dealing with CLL or any type of cancer, you never know when the next will be. We all hope and pray that it never comes back. My words to you are that I hope you remain strong and fight until you can no longer wager this war. So for the time being do not be afraid to tell others how you are feeling. As you can tell, my run through the cancer garden has been quite colorful. Peace and love to you all.

------ Look Ma We Did It-------

www.ingramcontent.com/pod-product-compliance
Lightning Source LLC
Chambersburg PA
CBHW061303040426
42444CB00010B/2495